THE HORRORS OF COLOR

THE DARK CARNIVAL

A COLORING BOOK FOR ADULTS

KATE TAYLOR DESIGN

This book features 40 intricate illustrations. Each illustration is printed on one side of the page, providing a convenient and enjoyable coloring experience for adults.

If you would like to reorder, please scan the QR Code

THE DARK CARNIVAL is a

thrilling addition to the "The Horrors of Color" series. This horror-themed coloring book is filled with twisted, sinister clowns, creepy carnival attractions, and a variety of other dark characters that come to life through the act of coloring. The intricate illustrations offer a unique and exciting coloring experience, allowing the reader to explore the dark side of their imagination. Whether you're a seasoned coloring enthusiast or just looking for a new form of self-expression, "The Dark Carnival" is sure to offer hours of entertainment and artistic satisfaction

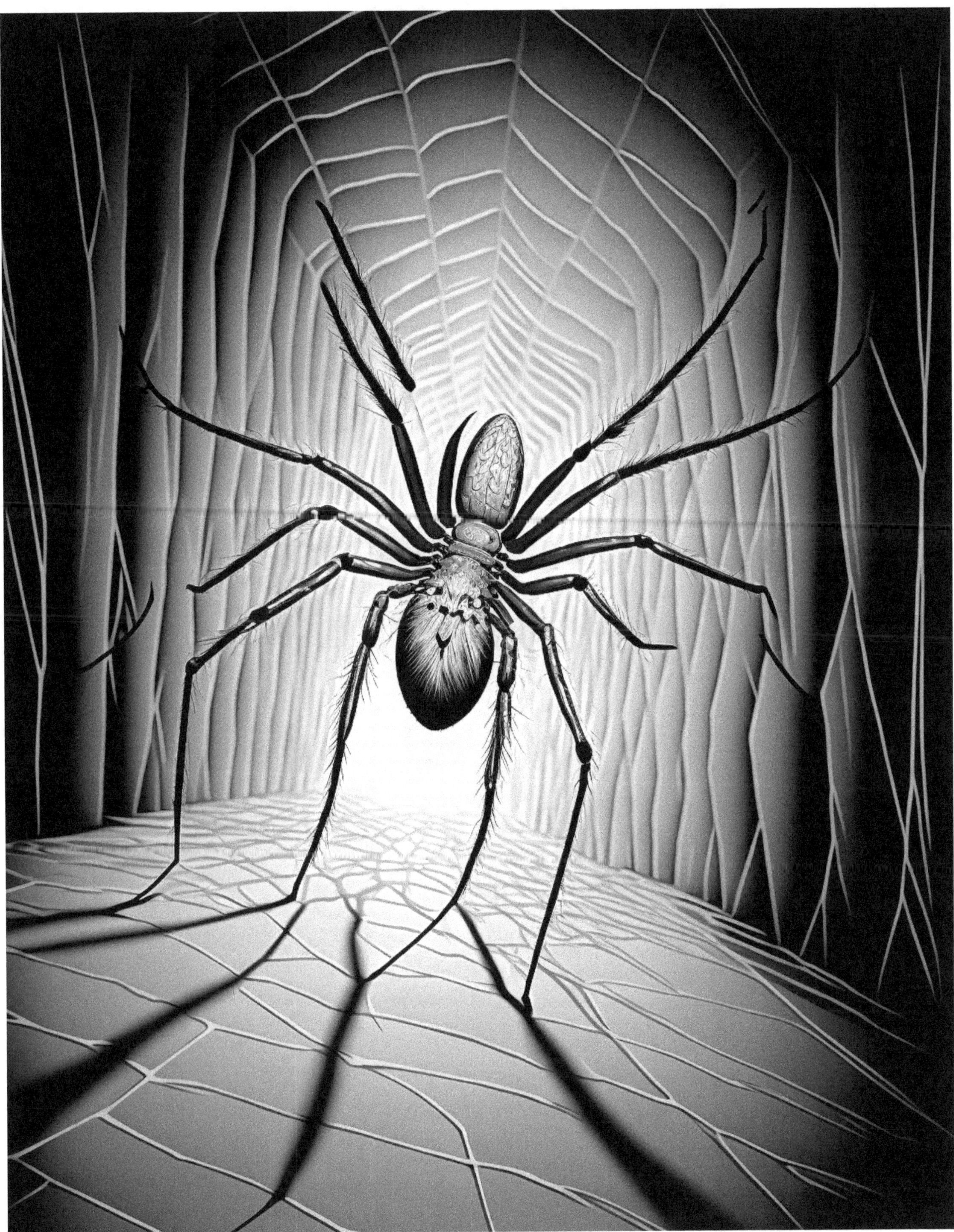

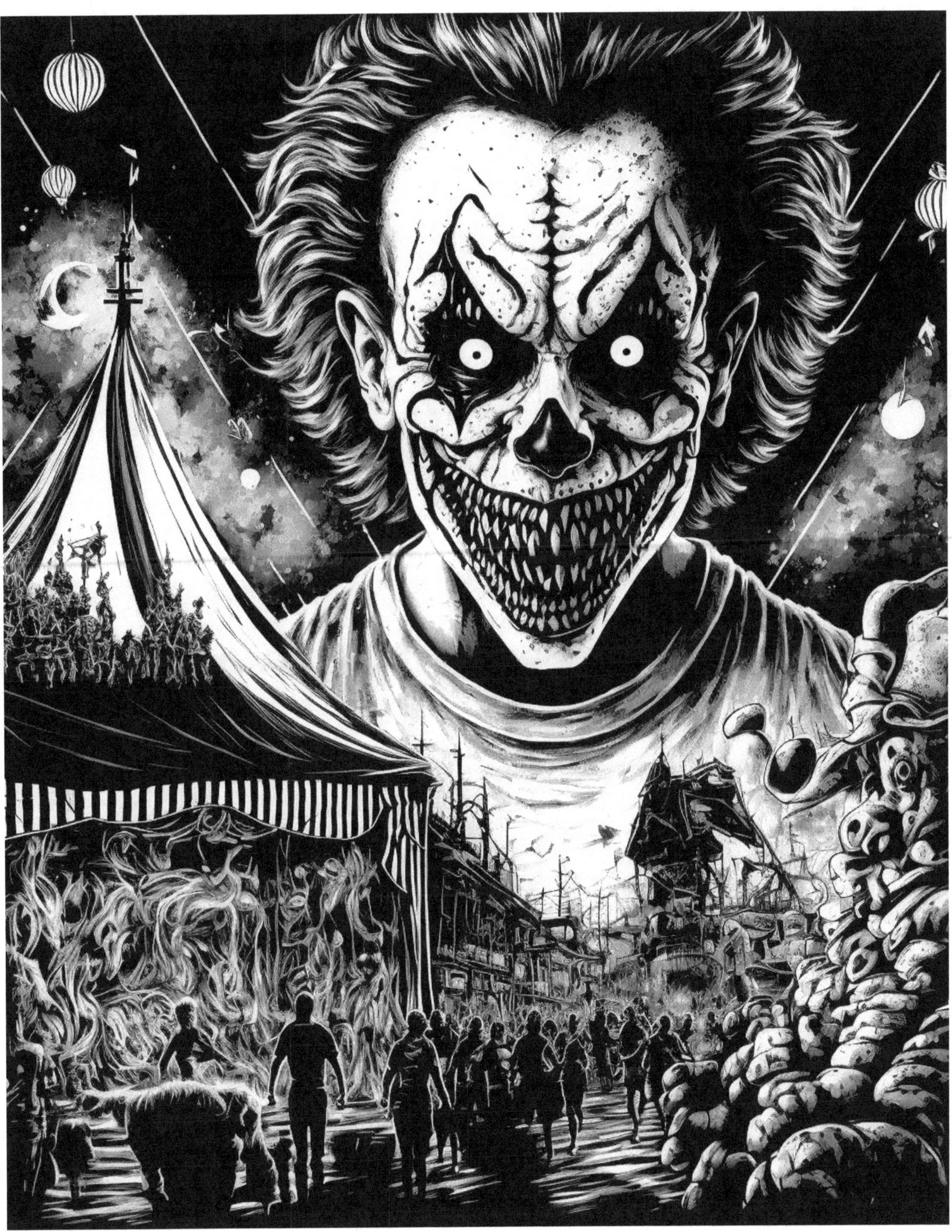

KATE TAYLOR DESING

OTHER COLORING BOOKS:

MYSTICAL CREATURES

- A Dragon Coloring Book for Adults
- A Unicorn Coloring Book for Adults
- A Phoenix Coloring Book fo Adults
- A Fairy Coloring Book for Adults
- A Mermaid Coloring Book for Adults
- A Goblin Coloring Book for Adults
- A Gnome Coloring Book for Adults
- A Troll Coloring Book for Adults
- A Gryphon Coloring Book for Adults

VEHICLES

- American muscle cars coloring book for kids
- Supercars coloring book for kids
- Antique car coloring book for kids
- Jumbo cars coloring book for kids
- Motorcycle Coloring book for kids

THE HORRORS OF COLOR

- The Dark Carnival: A Coloring Book for Adult
- The Haunted Mansion: A Coloring Book for Adults
- The Curse of the Mummy: A Coloring Book for Adults
- Horror coloring book

MANDALAS AND PATTERNS

- Geometric shapes and patterns coloring book
- Adult coloring book tessellations patterns
- Adult coloring book geometric patterns
- Adult coloring book circular patterns.
- 150 Mandala coloring book

QUOTES

- Inspirational quotes from the bible coloring book
- Money quotes coloring book
- Quotes for success coloring book
- Funny Mom Quotes and Patterns coloring book
- Motivational swear words coloring book

CHILDREN

- The Toddler Coloring Book

- Unicorn Coloring Book

- Dinosaur Coloring Book

- Mermaid Coloring Book

- Kawaii Friends Coloring Book

OTHER

- Flower coloring book

- Reverse coloring book

Scan the QR Code